Thrive in Law School!

A Friendly Guide to the Most Important Educational Experience of Your Life

By

Jeremy M. Stipkala, Ph.D., J.D.

To Andrew and Aviva:
May you succeed
no matter how you are called.

Persimmon Woods Press, LLC

Paperback ISBN 978-0-9997997-6-5

eBook ISBN 978-0-9997997-7-2

Table of Contents

I. Introduction

Congratulations! Welcome to law school! You are about to embark on the most important educational (and professional and perhaps personal growth) experience of your life so far. This law school adventure will resemble in some ways your college experience: you will take courses, earn grades, and progress toward a degree. But this will be *different*. Law school resembles college the way college resembled high school. New and seemingly impossibly complex material will challenge you to digest and deftly employ it. Novel ways of thinking, speaking, and even acting will be thrust upon you. And, at the end of it, you will be called Lawyer, Counselor, Attorney at Law: **Juris Doctor**.

Sounds impressive, doesn't it? Can you handle it? Dear Reader, I tell you emphatically **YES YOU CAN!** You have conquered college. Do you remember how difficult college appeared at first? No more spoon-feeding by friendly high school teachers. No-one telling you when to go to class, or when to do your homework, or even *how* to do your homework. No more classes with all of your friends – every class seemingly filled with strangers. Think back now to your freshman year in college. What if you had to take those classes again? How *easy* would that be? How about high school? Piece of cake! One day (next year), you will look down your nose at those poor "1L" (first-year) law students, and scoff at their deer-in-the-headlights expressions, as you will have mastered by then what they must face.

But before you do all that looking down your nose and scoffing (and I urge you to be gentle, even generous, with those who come behind you), you have to survive your First Day Of Law School. And then your Second Day Of Law School. And then your, umm, well, you get the idea. It is my hope and goal that this book, with its friendly voice, gives you insight into what comes next, and provides you with some tools that really help you thrive in law school and ultimately triumph in your study and practice of the law.

II. What to Expect In Lecture

A. Look to Your Right; Look to Your Left

Just before my first day of law school, I attended an orientation lecture in the university's grand auditorium. The law school dean, an august man with flaming red hair, came out to address the assembled cohort of fresh new law students. "Ladies and gentlemen," he said. "Look to your right; look to your left. Everyone you see here today, **you will see them at graduation**." A sigh of relief rippled across the auditorium, and morphed into an eruption of heart-felt applause. *We were all going to make it!*

A friend of mine told me of his law school orientation at a different law school. His dean gave the same instruction. "Look to your right; look to your left." But what that dean said next had a much different effect. "At the end of this academic year, *ten percent of you will be gone*." (That school had a policy of failing out ten percent of its incoming class.) I can only imagine the collective anxiety in that auditorium rocketing up to fever pitch. Students nervously glanced about, wondering if they were going to make it, or if they were going to number among the sacrificed in that decimated class of new law students.

What your law school dean says to you at orientation has a profound effect on you, apparently. My friend became such an effective student fighting for his academic survival. I met him taking an advanced class, Patent Licensing, while I was finishing my law degree and he was earning his LLM in intellectual property law at my law school. When we got together to study for the final exam in May, he could recite from his notes the exact dialogue between the professor and certain students from a lecture that happened *in February*. He even caught the nuanced variation the professor threw at the students, and the subtly different outcome that variation caused. I earned my only A+ in law school in that class, and I owe so much to that friend and his fierce skills as a law student.

In contrast, let me tell you about a classmate who was told that we would all be there at graduation. At the end of my second-to-last semester, I was good. I mean *really good*. As a "4L" – a fourth-year evening law student – I had mastered this law school thing, and I could eat a final exam for lunch. This course was Environmental Law, and the final exam was open book. I had my casebook and my book of statutes flagged with little yellow tongues of plastic, each flag marked in pencil with the name of a case or statute. Nervously awaiting the beginning of the exam, I tried to relax as much as I could. (I was *good*, but I'm still human.)

The student in front of me suddenly spun around and asked me, "Do you think we will have to discuss the statute on this exam?" Before I could stop myself, my eyes fell to my statute book, with all of its neat yellow flags ready to reveal the precise words of each statute to me. His eyes followed mine down, down, down to my statute book, and a look of horror seized his face. Trying my best to keep this awful moment from getting any worse for him, I said, "Oh, I might mention the statute if it comes up." He spun back around, more distressed than before. Suddenly, surprisingly, I felt very relaxed.

Take away a couple of things from these tales, Dear Reader. First and foremost, whether you conquer law school is in your hands. Your dean, perhaps, can help you do that by giving you a proverbial kick in the pants. But if anyone tells you that you will graduate no matter what, **ignore them**. (I think our dean's comments made too many students relax too much.) Instead imagine that they told you the opposite, if that helps to motivate you. You probably will graduate, but that does not mean your legal education will be worth much if you do not put in the effort. Second, do not worry about my friend's ability to capture verbatim what was said in lecture. You do not need that skill. I never developed it. No professor will ask you on the final exam: "Repeat exactly what I said in that lecture three months ago." And no client will ever ask you, "Precisely what did your professor say in the twelfth lecture of your Patent Licensing course?" I've been serving clients for twenty years, and the dialogue of that lecture just hasn't come up yet. So let's get real, and let me tell you what to expect and how to succeed.

B. So What Is Law School All About?

Law school has a rather simple structure. Most courses teach you a substantive area of the law – both the knowledge of what the law is, and how to analyze a set of circumstances in light of that law. Let me illustrate. Suppose you are learning about the law governing what happens when someone terminates the life of another someone. (I know – the law often delves into humanity at its worst.) The governing statute is, say, "Thou shalt not kill." The first case you read will reveal a good old fashioned premeditated murder most foul. Cain kills Abel, but in modern times where a court case provides the murderer with due process. The next case will involve a crime of passion, where a spouse catches her beloved in The Act, and suddenly The Bad, Bad Thing happens – without premeditation. The next case will involve a killing in self-defense, and the next case after that will involve an accidental killing. The next case after that will involve an attempted murder. And so on. Law school presents a statute and then a series of cases implicating the statute, thereby illustrating how the statute applies in a wide variety of real-life situations. At the end of your course, you would have a good feel for what kinds of killing violate the murder statute, and which do not.

Referring to my final exam on Environmental Law, we would explore a statute, say, the Clean Water Act. There, the statute says, "Thou shalt not dump thy toxic waste into thyne lakes and rivers." (I paraphrase.) The cases we studied explored the meaning and application of that statute, such as, for example, what does "dump" mean? What if something leaks by accident? What exactly is "toxic waste?" What if I just dump something nasty on the ground, and groundwater causes the nastiness to leech into a nearby river – did I still violate the statute? (You betcha!)

Another point about the law. Law has a certain hierarchy. Usually, the hierarchy starts with the Constitution at the top, passes through Congress making laws known as statutes, and ends with courts interpreting those statutes. If the courts reach results unintended by Congress or unpopular with the people, Congress can go back and change the language of the statute. (Remember "checks and balances" from civics class? Yeah! It's a thing.) Also relevant are regulations promulgated (how's that for a 50-cent word?) by administrative agencies.

How does that hierarchy work? Take the Clean Water Act. The Constitution gives Congress the power to regulate interstate commerce. Water flows among the states and impacts interstate commerce. Pollution from one state floating downriver to another state can severely impact the economy of the down-river state. (I am serious. The expansive interpretation of the Commerce Clause in our Constitution means Congress has broad power to pass laws on all kinds of things.) So Congress has the power to address water pollution because of the

Commerce Clause of the U.S. Constitution. Hence Congress passes a law (statute) that says, "Thou shalt not dump thy toxic waste into thyne lakes and rivers." (Again, I paraphrase.) The president, charged with carrying out the laws, creates a federal agency called the Environmental Protection Agency. The EPA studies the Clean Water Act and promulgates (there's that word again!) a regulation that says, "Waste water flowing from a factory into a lake or river shall contain no more than five parts per million of mercury." With that regulation in place, Jane Factory Owner can now test her waste water and see how much mercury it contains. Above five parts per million, she violates the regulation and probably the statute. Below five parts per million, she's golden. Properly-promulgated regulations have the force of law. And they save Congress from having to legislate the fine details like how much mercury in waste water is too much.

State law and local law have a similar hierarchy. (When looking at state law, an additional question arises: Does federal law pre-empt the state legislature from legislating in this area? But I digress.)

Why am I telling you this? Because a good deal of the cases addressing a statute address how the statute was passed. If Congress did not have the power to pass the statute, the statute is "unconstitutional." (Ever hear that word before?) Similarly, if the EPA did not have the authority to regulate the amount of mercury in factory waste water, then the regulation is unlawful. Also, if the procedure followed in the promulgation of the regulation was flawed, the regulation might not have the force of law behind it.

Another point about the law. Sometimes law comes from the court, and not Congress (or your state legislature). Imagine two people suing each other in court. "She stole my picture of my cat from my social media post, and passed it off as her own!" comes the allegation. Clearly, one party feels aggrieved by the actions of the other party, but let us suppose that Congress has not had a chance yet to legislate about pictures of cats posted on social media on the Internet. Not to worry. The court can still address the grievance, by pointing to previous cases involving similar principles. "When someone copies pictures from the social media postings of another, and passes the copied pictures as her own online, she violates established copyright law as if the copying were done in print," the court might conclude. But notice: in articulating that sentence, the court *made new law*. Suppose no-one ever addressed copying on the Internet before. By concluding that online copying is just like old-fashioned hardcopy copying, the judge extended the law into a new area of human activity. This new law is called **common law**.

Common law allows our system of legal governance to extend into new areas, perhaps long before our legislatures can get to those areas. Sometimes legislation never touches an area well-settled by the common law. More frequently, though, legislatures enact a statute that recites the Rule of Law developed in the courts to avoid any confusion. (Ha!)

There is another hierarchy in the law. If the Supreme Court of the United States says that "A" is the law, then, my goodness gracious, by all means know that "A" is the law (unless and until Congress says otherwise). If an appellate court, having jurisdiction over the geographical area where a case is being heard, has spoken on a subject (that is, written a judicial opinion deciding a case), that pronouncement is **controlling authority**. (The Supreme Court also provides controlling authority, you betcha.) If an appellate court from another circuit or another state has spoken on a subject, and there is no *controlling authority* on that subject in your circuit or state, then the neighboring appellate court provides **persuasive authority**. Your judge *must* adhere to controlling authority, and *should pay attention to* persuasive authority, but is free (within limits) to make up a brand-new Rule of Law in the absence of controlling authority.

There is one more point about the law you should know. "The law" has a division between criminal law and civil law. Criminal law, usually codified in statutes by the legislature, represents the people, society, the government suing a person for committing a crime. Civil law, in contrast, represents two private parties suing each other. Statutes may give private parties a "cause of action," or a cause of action may arise from the common law. Often, criminal law and civil law arise in the same transaction or occurrence. Kill someone, and the state prosecutes you under the criminal statutes outlawing murder, and you are punished by going to jail. Then, the family of the murder victim sues you for wrongful death, a civil cause of action. Or, you run a stop sign and cause a fender bender. A cop writes you a ticket for violating the traffic law set forth in a statute, technically a crime (a misdemeanor or minor crime, I will note). Then, the victim of the fender bender sues you in civil court for negligence for the damages she suffered.

An aside: a felony, generally speaking, is a crime punishable by a year or more in jail. A misdemeanor is a crime punishable by less than a year in jail. Some jurisdictions define the difference by statute, so there is no confusion as to whether a person has status as a felon.

The foregoing just barely touches on the beautiful structure of the law. I hope it whets your appetite to learn more. And, I hope my exposition of it helps prepare you for law school or at least what I say next.

C. Right Tools for the Job

Before I say what I am going to say next, I have to mention some tools you should acquire. The first tool you should get: a sound legal dictionary. Get the app and put it on your phone. Or get a hardcopy and put it on your desk. Among law dictionaries, *Black's Law Dictionary* represents the gold standard. Published since 1891, the current iteration is cited as *Black's Law Dictionary* (10th ed. 2014). The law contains an enormous vocabulary and a vast array of concepts, and you will do well to learn the relevant words and concepts quickly. Be careful, however, because every law student gets accused of overusing the new vocabulary (I got called out for this at an annual performance review at my law firm!) But take heart – the poor slobs in medical school think they have symptoms of every new disease they study – so it could be worse!

Another tool is *The Bluebook: A Uniform System of Citation* (Columbia Law Review Ass'n et al. eds., 20th ed. 2015). This book will help you cite cases and statutes in accordance with the most-widely accepted citation system in the country. This book, or a counterpart, will form part of your required reading first semester, so do not buy it the summer before law school until you know that *The Bluebook* will be the system taught at your law school.

A third tool, or class of tools, can be called summaries, hornbooks, or commercial outlines. Sometimes a single laminated sheet of paper, other times a small paperback book of a few hundred pages, those commercial outlines really can orient your thinking about an area of the law. They boil down the Rules of Law for a given area, and even summarize the key cases and historical development of the doctrines. I used these commercial outlines especially when an area of the law lacked all structure in my befuddled mind. Purchase these if and when you find the casebook, with its great volume of words, and the lecture, with its unique brand of theater, fail to clearly teach you what you need to know.

D. The Dreaded Socratic Method

Now that you know all about the law, and you have at least *Black's Law Dictionary* (or a fine counterpart), let's explore what law school lectures feel like.

Socrates was this ancient Greek guy who asked a lot of questions. A student would come to him seeking knowledge, and old Socrates would answer a question with a question. And follow up with more questions. By asking questions, Socrates sought to guide the student to greater understanding by forcing the student to reason through answers to Socrates's questions.

Today, it is a celebrated technique for law professors to ask questions of their students. Among other things, this strongly encourages students to prepare for lecture. Also, it forces students to participate in lecture. A professor can drone on and on for an hour or two and not really know whether anyone in the room is listening. But if she starts calling on students to answer questions, she will know exactly who has read the cases and who is paying attention to the lecture.

In most cases, the professor uses the Socratic method simply to engage the students. Lectures become an enlightening exchange, a conversation. Rarely does a professor embarrass or destroy a student; if the student gets embarrassed, it is because the student did not read the material before lecture. Think about it: a professor has so much material to cover, and does not advance her mission if she is wasting time beating up on an unprepared student. So a good professor will engage a student with astute questions, and nimbly shift to another student when the first student has reached the end of her understanding. It is no problem that a student eventually fails to answer One More Question. But how do you avoid an awful experience when the professor calls on you? Preparation!

III. How to Prepare for Lecture

A. Reading and Outlining Cases

Make friends with your syllabus, a veritable roadmap for your daily progress through a course. The only scary thing about the syllabus is the number of pages you have to read before each lecture. Initially, it will take your breath away. But things gets really scary if you fall behind. Hit the ground running and work hard to get through those pages before each lecture.

Do not, however, read those pages and pages of case law the way you might read a novel for pleasure. It will put you to sleep, I am sure. I am sure, because it put me to sleep. You have to shake up your mind and look for key parts of the case to keep yourself alert, even entertained, to get through all those pages. Eventually, you will become better at reading a case so that you can zero in on the key parts quickly, and absorb what you need for lecture. Soon, you may even find yourself hunting for nerd-crack in the pages of your case book.

These are the key parts of any case:

Venue
Posture
Key Facts
Issue
Holding

Let's examine each one.

Venue is the court in which the case is being decided. It could be a district court, which is where trials with juries (and sometimes without juries – "bench trials") are held. One side wins and one side loses, and the loser appeals the case to an appellate court. The appellate court usually addresses questions of law, and ensures that the district court or trial court followed all of the proper procedures. Then, there is the Supreme Court. The Supreme Court does not have to take every case, and selects only those cases (from the appellate court level) with compelling legal questions needing the best legal minds to sort out what the law is. Other possible venues include administrative courts and, rarely for law school purposes, arbitration or mediation venues.

Posture means the procedural history of the case. If a district court or trial court provides the venue, does the court provide the first hearing of the case, or did the case go up on appeal and come back down on "remand?" If the venue is the appellate court, is this the case's first visit to the appellate court? If an appeal, who won below? Who lost, and why? Does the decision articulate the standard of review for facts found below (often reversed only for "clear error") and for conclusions of law made below (usually "de novo" or brand-new review from scratch)?

Key Facts determine the outcome of the case. "Who, what, why, where, when, and how," and what is the legal significance? What facts are alleged, and what facts are proven or found? Note that the court will "find" facts, as opposed to "conclude" matters of law. "I *find* that the light was red proven by evidence beyond a reasonable doubt, so I *conclude* that the defendant was guilty of the moving violation as a matter of law."

Issues means the question or questions the court addresses. Why are we having this case? Are the parties arguing about facts ("The light was red!" "No! The light was green!") or law ("The plaintiff was contributorily negligent, so the law says the defendant doesn't owe the plaintiff so much.") Often, a case must address multiple issues to reach a conclusion. As you can guess, issues over the law are far more interesting to a law school lecture than issues over facts.

Holding means the decision the court reached. "Party X wins because . . . ." "We hold for the defendant." "Defendant is not liable because . . . ." Or, more opaquely, "Sustained" or "Reversed." On appeal, if the appellate court agrees with the result reached below, the trial court's decision will be "sustained." If they disagree, the decision below will be "reversed." Sometimes, the case is "remanded," which means the court below has to look at some issue in accordance with the guidance provided by the appellate court. Also look for the Rule of Law. "When facts A are present, the law is B." This articulation of the Rule of Law guides others resolving future cases with similar facts.

When considering the holding, imagine the following dialogue with your professor. "Johnson! [Insert your name here.]" "Johnson! Wake up and tell us the holding in *Smith v. Jones*." [Professors are never such drill instructors. But it might feel that way the first time the professor bellows your name.] "Umm, [Party X] won," you rightly observe. "Why?" comes the inevitable, foreseeable rejoinder. **"[Party X] won because when [facts A] are present, the law is [B]."** Wait a second! You just stated the Rule of Law. The Words Of Law dripped from your tongue, and you showed the world (or at least the portion of your class paying attention) that You Can Think And Reason Like A Lawyer. Congratulations! The point, Dear Reader: endeavor to be prepared to articulate that Rule of Law for each case you read.

Other interesting tidbits include dissents and concurrences and policy discussions. A holding may say, "Party X wins because . . . ." A dissent says, "While a majority of the judges on the panel of judges hearing this case conclude that Party X *wins*, I disagree: I think Party X should *lose* because . . . ." A concurrence says, "I agree with the majority that Party X should win, but I think for *different* reasons." Policy discussions explore why the law is the way it is, or the way the law should be, or the legislative intent behind the passing of the law.

With practice, you should be able to gather the venue, posture, key facts, issues, and holding. Skimming the rest of the case decision, you should be able to spot whether there are any other interesting tidbits that might require a closer look. At first, you should consider writing out a case outline for each case. Then, eventually, annotations in your case book will help you find the key parts when the professor calls on you.

Let me go back to the holding, and show you the whole point of the study of law. "[Party X] won because when [facts A] are present, the law is [B]." Law is about the application of rules to facts. If a person intentionally kills another (fact), then that person is guilty of murder (rule). If you drive your car faster than the posted speed limit (fact), then you are guilty of speeding (rule). That, Dear Reader, is the grand premise, the cornerstone, the first building block, perhaps the whole building, of being a lawyer. **Determine the facts, then apply the law.** Who was driving? What was the speed limit? Was the speed limit posted? How fast was the car going? It matters not whether your car is red or blue, or whether your parents hail from a tropical island in the South Pacific. If you were driving your car over the speed limit, you were speeding. The law should feel like an inevitable, inexorable conclusion flowing from established facts.

Think of the statue of Lady Justice sometimes seen around courthouses. She holds the Scales Of Justice upon which each side places their evidence. Whoever has the weightier evidence, wins. She is blindfolded, so she ignores irrelevant facts, like whether your car is red or blue or whether you claim Pacific Islander heritage. And she grasps The Sword Of Justice, ready to slice off the portion each deserves. To me, the sword means that the law applies to us all equally. No-one is above the law, or beyond the reach of that blade, and we each get what we deserve under the law. That society is governed by law and the equal application of that law to all, to me, represent the *foundation of civilization*. I feel fortunate and honored to serve others guiding them with the law. How civilized!

Now back to preparing for lecture. You know that you are ready for lecture if you can do one simple thing: Can you summarize each case in the reading assignment using this formula: "[Party X] won because when [facts A] are present, the law is [B]?" That oversimplifies things a bit, because sometimes there are many other issues. But let me say this: if you *cannot* summarize a case according to that formula, you have not yet fully comprehended the case.

Notice, Dear Reader, that you may have to dig a little bit to get to the point of a case. "Defendant is charged with speeding," you read. "Ah! This case is about the rule governing speeding," you may suppose. But keep reading. Any number of issues could be dispositive (that is, control the outcome of the case), from whether the charges were being brought in the proper court to whether the speed limit was properly posted. Similarly, the authors of your case book may have included a case to make a certain point that is not neatly aligned with the main thrust of the case. So keep an open mind as you hunt for the holding.

In law school, I would work hard to read all the cases the professor assigned before each lecture. (That means I didn't always manage to read all the cases. That means I prayed that I would not be called on when we reached the cases I hadn't read.) When I was well prepared and Life hadn't stopped me from reading every case, I had annotated each case, the annotations indicating venue, posture, key facts, issues, and holdings. Then, a few minutes before lecture, I would review each case, looking for those critical parts of each case. Naively confident, I would stride into lecture and take my seat.

B. Now Organize All That Stuff!

During lecture, I would take notes by hand. I had selected the smoothest-writing pen I could, and made sure I had plenty of yellow legal pads with three holes punched in the left margin. Later, I would keep these pages in a three-ring binder. Whether you take notes with a pen on paper or on a laptop is up to you. If I had to do it again, I might consider using a laptop, if only because your work product is easy to reorganize and to search. Plus now I am a much faster typist!

My notes sought to capture whatever the professor emphasized. I would write the case name, to orient my notes to my case book. And then I would write what I could glean from the discussion. You've been to college; your own note-taking style should be well honed by now. Use that style if it works for you. A key change in my note-taking style for me, and a useful technique for you, is to find the opportunity to critically review your notes *within a half-hour* of finishing lecture. During this post-lecture review, your memory of the discussion will be fresh and you will be able to fill in gaps in your notes. I used this review to add legibility to my hastily-scribbled notes. If you wait till the end of the semester to look at your notes, you will find illegible words offering you no clue to their significance, and major gaps omitting key points.

At some point, you may want to prepare an outline. Yes, the fabled outline. To distinguish from other outlines I will discuss below, let us call this outline "the substantive outline." A substantive outline of a course has two purposes, at least. One purpose is to create an organized reference tool covering the entire course. The other purpose is to get the knowledge to stick to you. Knowledge is a lot like dirt. You have to move it around, play with it, get it all over you, and then it will stick to you. So preparing a substantive outline organizes

30

the material for reference, and gets it to stick to you. Funny, your substantive outline should vaguely resemble the syllabus, only with a lot more detail.

I did not always prepare a substantive outline for my classes. My notes represented my substantive outline. For some students, the substantive outline they prepare represents and incorporates the notes they take in lecture. If it helps you to retain the knowledge by preparing a substantive outline, by all means, do so. But know that the final exam does not ask you to prepare an outline. So how to study for the final exam?

IV. Final Exams

A. Format

One chief difference between college and law school is the testing. In college, you have so many tests during the semester. Sometimes, you do not have to take the final exam in college if your grades on the tests given during the semester were high enough. In law school, however, your entire grade for the semester depends on the final exam. This make-or-break test format causes much consternation among law students.

I remember my first law school final exam. I had studied hard (I will tell you how to study momentarily), and confidently (naively?) strode into the lecture hall for the exam. My first breath of air inside the lecture hall eroded my confidence, however, because the sense of doom was *palpable*. My fellow students were freaking out! The passengers on the Titanic probably held more hope in their hearts. What surprised me was how infectious the panic seemed! Some students were clearly anxious, and that would have been expected. But I could not have foretold that even usually-confident and well-prepared students had a kind of buggy look in their eyes, nervously gawking about. Knots of students chattered frantically about this doctrine or that case, and this caused the panic to spread. I felt it too. Did we all forget what our dear dean told us? Yet if you looked to your right, looked to your left, all you could see were first-year law students in various states of terror. Mercifully, the exam began soon enough and we all *somehow* made it to graduation.

What does a law school exam look like? The happy news is that some professors let you see well beforehand. The library, or the professors themselves, make past exams available for students to peruse. Sometimes, the past exams include answers, and that really helps you understand what the professor seeks with a given question. Be sure that you are *authorized* to obtain a past exam before you do, so you don't get accused of cheating.

Even if your professor does not make past exams available, know that your syllabus will appear on your final exam. The syllabus may be mixed up and disguised as a series of difficult questions. But think about it. How does Jane Q. Professor write the final exam? She pulls out the syllabus and begins dreaming up fact patterns.

The format itself is fairly straightforward. (I am talking about essays, not short-answer questions or multiple-choice questions, which sometimes appear. Those are even more straightforward.) One or more fact patterns appear, each with one or more questions at the bottom. A bunch of stuff happens; somebody gets sued; what is the outcome? The student's job is to write an essay that clearly answers the question, applying the law to the facts. Generally speaking, "all" of the material covered in the course appears on the final exam, so the student should be prepared to study the entire scope of material covered by the course.

Essay questions, as they are called, can be tested on a computer or on paper. Sometimes, the professor will pick the format; other times, you can request to type or to hand-write your answers. If a laptop will be used, you will be asked to download software that sequesters everything else on your computer. Whether to type or to write, if it is up to you, depends on your comfort levels. Can you type quickly? Is your handwriting at least a little legible? Whatever you do, be sure to practice writing essays under timed conditions in your chosen format.

But I am getting ahead of myself! How *do* you study for a final exam in law school?

B. How to Study

First, get an idea of the scope of material covered in the course. How much of the syllabus did the professor teach? Did she cover anything not on the syllabus? Hopefully, your class notes reveal all the material that will appear on the exam. Can you write a list of all the Rules of Law that you learned from the reading and from lecture? Can you identify the policy considerations that drive any of those rules?

Second, devise a way to get the material into your brain. Usually, this focusses on the Rules of Law. Let me take an example rule and illustrate how I absorbed the material. Consider the rule for negligence: "A person is negligent if that person owes another person a duty, breaches that duty, and causes injury to that other person." Notice that the rule has elements. Each element represents a set of facts that, if absent, foreclose the applicability of that Rule of Law to the facts at hand. Suppose there is no breach, or there is no injury. In that case, there can be no negligence. So break your Rules of Law into elements – "Negligence: duty, breach, causing, injury." Or, equivalently, "Negligence: duty, breach, causation, damages." Write down the Rules of Law, every one, that you learned in class, and let your syllabus guide you in the organization of related rules.

I would create a **"memorization outline"** as follows. On a piece of legal-sized (*of course*) notebook paper, I would write in the left-hand margin:

Negligence:
Duty
Breach
Causation
Damages

I used a pen with the finest point I could find, and wrote small, neat block print so I could fit the most information on a page. I would do that for every Rule of Law that we learned for the entire course. When that was complete, I had a column of about two inches wide with all of the Rules of Law running down the page. I would build this memorization outline until I had all the substantive rules for the entire course captured. (Often this took several pages.) Then, I would write the elements of the rules again, this time in a column just to the right of the first column. I would peek at the first column as needed. The second column repeated the rules and elements from the first column. Then I would do it again in a third column, then a fourth. While writing each successive column, I would work hard to peek less and less. By the time I was writing the fifth column, I had the rules and their elements memorized. Then, on the exam, I could write next to the question that raised an issue of negligence: "Neg: Duty, Breach, Cause, Dam." Once that happened, I felt like the right answer was already on the page.

Let's talk policy. Sometimes policy considerations drive a Rule of Law, and those policies appear on the exam. Let me illustrate using negligence. In life, there is a person who is the "cheapest cost avoider." The cheapest cost avoider has to work the least to avoid or remedy a particular bad outcome. Consider a hockey stadium. Behind each goal, there exists a considerable danger of pucks travelling at high speed entering the spectators' area and injuring spectators. If a 90-mile-an-hour slapshot hits a spectator, the damage could be substantial. So how do we avoid that damage? Each person who chooses to sit behind a goal can wear a goalie's mask, helmet, and padding, and thereby avoid injury. Suppose that kit costs each spectator $100. Or, the stadium owner could erect a large net sufficient to catch the errant pucks behind each goal at a cost of $1,000. Yes, a kit for $100 costs less than a net costing $1,000, but notice that dozens of spectators would have to spend that $100.

The cheapest cost avoider doctrine imposes the burden for avoiding an injury on the actor or actors who could avoid the injury at the cheapest cost to society overall. Thus, a $1,000 net is the preferred mitigation, compared to dozens of spectators spending collectively thousands and thousands of dollars to address the same risk. So when Johnny Spectator gets smashed in the nose at the hockey game and sues the stadium owner, will we let the stadium owner argue that Johnny assumed the risk and should have been wearing protective gear? No, according to the cheapest cost avoider policy. The stadium owner should have installed the net. In other words, "the stadium owner had a **duty** to protect Johnny Spectator from the foreseeable injury Johnny suffered. The owner **breached** that duty by failing to install a net. That breach **led directly to** Johnny being injured, which caused **damages** in the form of medical bills, pain, and suffering for Johnny. Therefore, the stadium owner is liable to Johnny for negligence." (Can you see yourself writing that answer on your final exam? More importantly for today's discussion, can you see how I applied the facts to each element of the Rule of Law about negligence?) Now here's where you introduce policy into your answer for more points: "This result makes sense, because the stadium owner is the cheapest cost avoider; that is, the stadium owner could have installed a net at a cost of $1,000 and prevented Johnny's injury, while not requiring the dozens of spectators sitting behind the goals to each purchase and wear $100 kits of protective gear." Ahh! You have added a little policy to your answer.

How do you get the necessary policy doctrines into your brain? Your memorization outline! Add to your memorization outline any policy doctrines you might need, such as, for example:

Cheapest Cost Avoider:

Actor who can
avoid or mitigate risk
at lowest cost to society.

Write out your memorization outline
several times over the course of a few days
right before your exam, and it will sink in.

Once the memorization outline of
substantive doctrines (and a few policy
concepts) was completed, I would also
produce a **case list**. Often, I formed this list
in the same format as the memorization
outline, since I would endeavor to memorize
(or at least internalize) it as well. Each entry
would be very concise, having only the case
name, a key fact, and the holding, such as,
for example:

Smith v. Jones – Car accident.
Violate traffic statute = evidence of breach
of duty for negligence.

Once I completed the **case list
including the name, key fact, and
holding**, I would write out that list maybe
twice more, not so much as to *memorize* the
list, but to help me *recall* a case or two on
the final exam. Making this case list and

writing it out a couple of times accomplished two things for me. First, it helped me learn the material of the course by looking at it from a slightly different perspective. Forcing me to boil down each case to such a concise entry on the case list really helped me synthesize the copious verbiage of each decision into a neat little take-home message. Second, the case list got me more points on the final exam, as I could sprinkle case names into my answers. I used case names like spice – a little bit here, and a little bit there; I did not drown my essays with case names. Where the professor obviously riffed off a case from the reading to create a fact pattern, it provided easy extra points to throw in a sentence or two that started, "This case presents facts similar to <u>Smith v. Jones</u>, where . . . ." (I would underline case names in my answers, because handwritten italics just didn't work with my hen-scratch handwriting.)

You can use the cases to support your essay by pointing out similarities or differences in facts and outcomes. Watch carefully for differences in the facts; for example, in *Smith v. Jones*, it could be that the defendant had violated a traffic law and therefore was found to have breached her duty to drive reasonably; on your final exam, your defendant could have been found to be driving within the traffic laws (the speed limit, say). Students' final exam essays that discern differences in facts possibly leading to different outcomes provide nerd-crack for professors, and higher grades for the students!

As you are learning or memorizing the material for the exam, be sure to **PRACTICE**. No exam ever asked students to write an outline, or to just recite from memory every Rule of Law and policy doctrine covered in lecture. So you have to practice writing essays. That means you have to get practice questions from somewhere. Past exams (lawfully obtained!), hypotheticals presented in lecture, and even commercial sources can provide practice questions. Feel free to make up your own fact patterns, too. And then practice writing out your essays.

C. Issue Spotting

It will be a Bad Day At Law School if a question on the final exam asks (begs?) you to address one issue, but you address a completely different issue. Take the *Smith v. Jones* case above, in which a violation of a traffic statute provides evidence of a breach of duty for a negligence case. If your essay dives into the intricacies of the defendant's violation of the traffic statute, but fails to address whether the defendant was negligent (and you studied negligence all semester, not criminal traffic law), you may not receive any points. Let's take a look at a question, and see if we can spot the issue:

> Patty is driving her car down the street. She comes to an intersection with four-way stop signs, and comes to a complete stop. Then, as Patty proceeds through the intersection, her car is struck by Dotty's car, which did not stop before entering the intersection. Patty suffers a broken arm in the collision. A police officer

arrives on the scene, interviews Patty and Dotty and a couple of eye witnesses, and writes a ticket for Dotty for failing to stop at a stop sign. Patty sues Dotty. On what legal theory should Patty proceed?

First thing you might do is *look for the question*. "On what legal theory should Patty proceed?" Patty is suing Dotty. Patty is not, for example, pressing charges and asking the state to sue Dotty for Dotty's criminal act. So do not be misled by the very applicable criminal statute about running stop signs also at play in this case. Patty can sue Dotty on civil grounds, as opposed to criminal grounds, so what civil causes of action might Patty bring? "I know!" you exclaim. "Negligence!" And you hurriedly scribble "Neg: Duty, Breach, Cause, Dam" in the margin of this book. Then, if you recall it, the *Smith v. Jones* case might come to mind, or at least a vague memory of the holding that violating a criminal statute provides evidence of breaching a duty for negligence analysis.

The major issue of negligence is raised by the question. The minor issue of proving a breach of duty (one element of the negligence cause of action) is flagged by the police officer writing a ticket. This fact pattern flags one more minor issue that is slightly more important than the traffic ticket: whether Patty was *contributorily* negligent. (Don't worry if you did not see contributory negligence issue – it will come to you when you study the material.) Every good defense attorney will immediately look for contributory negligence; so too will every good law school student once they have taken the course. However, Patty came to a complete stop before entering the intersection, and *there is no evidence* that she was negligent in bringing about the accident. So a decent answer to the question above addresses Dotty's negligence. A very good answer also addresses the contributory negligence issue. A super duper answer ALSO addresses Dotty's violation of the statute as evidence of her breach of her duty to drive reasonably. A super duper very good awesome answer mentions *Smith v. Jones* by name, on top of all that.

How do you get good at issue spotting? Prepare by internalizing the Rules of Law you are studying; practice reading questions with fact patterns with the purpose of spotting the issues and answering the questions; and read the question *first* to orient yourself *before* you read the fact pattern. And practice issue spotting *during* the semester. Do not wait for the end of the semester to start building issue spotting skills. You will thank me later. Practice early and often! For your convenience, I restate:

How to Build Issue Spotting Skills:

Prepare
Practice
Read the Question First

D. All Elements Rule

It will be another Bad Day At Law School if you write your essay and go on and on about how Dotty breached her duty to drive reasonably, as shown by Dotty's violation of the stop-at-all-stop-signs law, but you forget to mention Patty's broken arm and bashed-up car, that is, the injuries or damages element of the negligence rule. Well, it won't be so bad, because you will still get some points, unlike the poor slob who proved up the traffic violation and did not mention negligence at all.

You must adhere to what I call **The All Elements Rule**. Lawyers live and thrive by this rule; cases are tossed out if not. Remember when you scribbled "Neg: Duty, Breach, Cause, Dam" above? (I will pause while you admire your First Rule Of Law.) Your answer on the final exam, and indeed every bit of work product you ever produce, must address each and every element of the applicable Rules of Law. Why? Because failing to prove up even one teeny weeny little element means the entire cause of action fails. That's how law works. In many countries, attorneys are thought of as clerks, and our work is thought of as clerical. That view of attorneys and the law is supported by the check-the-box nature of needing all of the elements to support a cause of action or meet a Rule of Law. (We are soooo much more than clerks, Dear Reader!) Commit to internalizing and implementing the All Elements Rule, and you will have taken Your First Step Toward Becoming A Real Live Attorney.

E. All Evidence Suggestion

When you prepare and eventually write your answer, you will want to employ all relevant facts and evidence. That means two things: first, not all facts and evidence are relevant. The fact pattern above is very lean; there are not too many (any?) irrelevant facts. Names, types of vehicles, time of day, etc., could be irrelevant. (Or they could be relevant if the defendant argues the sun was in her eyes, etc.) In a longer fact pattern, there could be more facts and evidence; importantly, there is no need to mention every single factoid. But **Do Not Ignore "Bad Facts."** A successful answer (and attorney) will address those facts and evidence that go against the conclusion the answer reaches. (You KNOW your opponent in court will DWELL on those facts and evidence that go against your conclusion, and the judge will HAMMER you if you ignore them.) Take a good, hard look at *all* the facts, including the "bad" facts, weigh them on the Scales Of Justice, and confirm that you are reaching the correct conclusion. If there are too many bad facts, maybe you *should* reach the opposite conclusion . . . .

Second, you do not want to make up evidence without extreme caution. It is a brilliant (partial) answer to say, "Patty came to a complete stop before entering the intersection. There is no evidence that Patty was contributorily negligent in causing the collision with Dotty's car." Only if you have some doctrine burning inside of you should you even consider suggesting different facts or evidence. For example, "If Patty were intoxicated, or there were other evidence of Patty's negligence, then Dotty might raise Patty's contributory negligence in causing the collision to reduce Dotty's potential liability to Patty." That should get you some points, especially if you saw no other way to introduce the concept of contributory negligence and just had to get it out there. (I prefer "there is no evidence" to "if there were [made-up evidence]" to support mentioning another Rule of Law.) In any case, please avoid sounding like this: "If aliens from outer space fired laser beams at Dotty's car and caused it to accelerate at half the speed of light into the intersection, Dotty could claim a break in the chain of causation and therefore Dotty would have no liability for negligence here."

F. Outline Your Answer – AIRAC

Now it is time to prepare your answer. How do you do that? Somewhere, on the pages of the test, on scratch paper, or on your laptop screen if you are typing your final exam, write a brief outline of your answer. I offer you a tool for organizing all of your answers, now and forever, in law school and beyond:

(I will pause while you play some dramatic music from your fave playlist.)

AIRAC. That stands for **Answer, Issue, Rule, Analysis, and Conclusion.** Okay, turn off the music so I can elaborate.

Answer. Answer the question. "Negligence" is the answer to the question above, "On what legal theory should Patty proceed?"

Issue. The main issue is whether Dotty was negligent in causing the collision with Patty's car. Only handle one issue at a time per AIRAC structure. Multiple issues get confusing. Other issues get their own AIRAC.

Rule. Recite the Rule of Law that governs the issue. Here you might scribble "Neg: Duty, Breach, Cause, Dam" in your outline if it is not adequately set forth already nearby (because you couldn't help spewing it out as soon as you saw it raised in the fact pattern).

Analysis. This is where you apply the law to the facts. It is very important to not make up stuff here. On *these* facts, with *this* evidence, are all of the elements of the

Rule of Law met? If "yes," plaintiff wins. If "no," defendant wins. Note that the *Smith v. Jones* doctrine is a part of proving negligence, because it relates to an element of negligence, breach of duty. So that doctrine is properly raised in your negligence analysis, not as a separate issue with its own AIRAC structure.

Conclusion. "Dotty is negligent because all of the elements of negligence are present."

Separately, do another AIRAC analysis for contributory negligence. Do not conflate the negligence analysis with the contributory negligence analysis, because it will be too confusing.

So your outline for the foregoing question might look like this:

A. [Answer] Dotty neg.

I. [Issue] Wr Dotty neg.

R. [Rule]. Neg:
   Duty

Breach – Smith v. Jones.
Cause
Dam

A. [Analysis]

C. [Conclusion]

[Then outline the minor issue of contributory negligence.]

A. [Answer] Patty not contrib. neg.

I. [Issue] Wr Patty contrib. neg.

R. [Rule] Neg: Duty, Breach, Cause, Dam *to self* [The rule for contributory negligence is *almost* the same as it is for negligence.]

A. [Analysis]

C. [Conclusion]

When you actually outline for the final exam, you need not write out all of the foregoing. You will get better with practice.

So practice early in the semester, and especially before final exams. Just don't wait to start practicing the day before finals begin!

Notice that "AIRAC-ing" suggests that you write the answer first. Often, however, your thought processes are not complete, so do not write your answer in your outline until you are certain of the answer! Sure, write "A I R A C" down the page, but start by writing the issue in your outline. Or, if the rule pops into your brain, start with writing the rule in your outline.

Also, note that I did not write anything next to "A" for analysis or "C" for conclusion. Write something if you need to. At least write "A" and "C" so you do not forget to do your analysis and conclusion!

A note about policy: If a policy discussion might gain you more points, be sure to note it in your outline. But be judicious. The cheapest cost avoider doctrine might be better applied elsewhere on the exam.

G. Write Your Answer

Here's what an answer might look like to the question set forth above. (Don't write [Answer], [Issue], etc. – I include it below so you can see AIRAC at work!) (I also include advance concepts like the standard of proof (preponderance of the evidence) and proximate causation – you will learn those in law school – I include them here for completeness.)

[Answer] Patty should proceed on the legal theory that Dotty was negligent in causing the collision with Patty's car. [Issue] The issue is whether Patty can prove Dotty was negligent. [Rule] Negligence requires a plaintiff to prove [by a preponderance of the evidence] that the defendant had a duty to the plaintiff, breached that duty, and [proximately] caused injury or damages to the plaintiff. [Analysis] Here, Dotty had a duty to drive reasonably. She breached that duty by entering the intersection without stopping at the stop sign. Violation of a traffic law provides evidence of the breach of duty. See Smith v. Jones. In that case, a defendant was held to have breached her duty to drive reasonably, as shown by an excessive speed that violated a traffic law. Here, the police officer reached the conclusion that Dotty had failed to stop at the stop sign, based on interviews with Patty, Dotty, and two eye witnesses. If the traffic citation for Dotty's failure to stop at the stop sign is upheld or not contested, that provides evidence of Dotty's breach of her duty to drive reasonably. Dotty's collision with Patty's car directly and foreseeably caused damage to Patty's car, and injury to Patty. Patty suffered a broken arm in the collision. [Conclusion] Accordingly, Dotty is liable to Patty on the legal theory of negligence.

[Issue] Another issue is whether Patty was contributorily negligent. [Answer] On these facts, she was not. [Rule] A plaintiff is contributorily negligent if the plaintiff owed a duty to the defendant, breached that duty, and [proximately] caused injury or damages to herself. [Analysis]. Here, Patty owed a duty to Dotty to drive reasonably. There is no evidence that Patty breached that duty in this case, since Patty came to a complete stop before entering the intersection. Since any injuries suffered by Dotty were not caused by any breach of duty by Patty, [conclusion] Patty is not contributorily negligent in this case.

There you go! Now just do that over and over for the next three or four years, and law school is in the bag!

H. Further Test Taking Skills

Manage your time!

Carefully manage your time. Do not do, as I did once in law school, and take thirty minutes to draft a beautiful essay on a ten-point question, unaware that there were forty more points to be had on the next page. I am sure I got all ten points!

Read the entire test first.

Reading the entire test (briefly) would have saved me from the foregoing goof-up. Make sure you know the instructions you have to follow, and quickly scan the entire test so you see how many questions you have to answer, the magnitude of each question, etc., so you can allocate your time appropriately.

Finish an answer and move on.

Fretting about a question for which you have no clue gets you nowhere. If you have allotted ten minutes for that question, then give it your all for ten minutes. Write all you can, with the best organization you can muster. Then, when that ten minutes finishes, move on to the next question. Forgetaboutit. It is time to get more points on another question, likely for which you know lots more.

Sprinkle in policy and case names carefully!

Notice how I did NOT throw the cheapest cost avoider doctrine into Patty and Dotty's little fender bender? Sure, Dotty could be the cheapest cost avoider in that situation, and society rightly imposes on her the cost of her negligence because she could have avoided the collision altogether if she just applied her brakes. But I would save that policy discussion for the question about the baseball game where the spectator gets hit by a foul tip behind home plate. That's a lot more similar to the hockey stadium situation, so it is probably more appropriate to deploy it in your answer to that question.

Also, mention case names when the facts are very similar. Okay, maybe you are a brainiac, and you can mention every case in every answer you write. But do not obscure your analysis with name dropping. Show the professor you know the cases, sure. But show your professor that you can analyze like a lawyer, too.

V. Legal Research and Writing

A. Pay Attention: You Will Need This Later

Dear Reader, this could be **The Most Important Chapter** in this entire book, because the skills you learn in your Legal Research and Writing course will serve you well for the rest of your legal career. (Good news! After graduation, you will *NOT* have to take final exams ever again!)

Speaking of final exams, some courses will require you to write a term paper for your grade, instead of taking a final exam. Embrace that requirement! Not only will your term paper written at your leisure absolve you of the stress of a final exam, but that term paper also could provide you with a writing sample for applying for "clerkships" (internships or apprenticeships with judges) and other jobs. And, law schools often require at least one course in which the grade is based on a term paper to graduate ("the writing requirement"). So this could be A Very Important Chapter indeed.

Not a day goes by that I do not look up a rule, a statute, or a case. Why? Because it is *important* to get the words exactly right. An agency, a legislature, or a panel of judges worked hard to get the language of the Rule of Law precisely where they wanted it. The least we can do is look up and read that language, right? I will give you an example, Dear Reader, in the form of a challenge. Can you recite the Ten Commandments? Can you at least name all ten, even if you cannot recite the exact words of each? Or, how about this: Can you recite the speed limit law, or the jay-walking law, or the you'd-better-pay-for-that-cup-of-coffee-or-you'll-go-to-jail law, or any of the laws that you may have implicated (or broken) today? (You flaunters of traffic laws *know who you are!*) Unless you have recently looked them up, you (most people, anyway) cannot recite many Rules of Law by heart with accuracy.

Another beautiful aspect of the law is that it changes *constantly*. You have numerous legislatures, agencies, local government councils, and judges whose *sole reason for existence* is to make more Rules of Law to tell you what to do. Rules and regulations are constantly morphing due to a wide variety of factors. Broadly speaking, we *know more* today than we did ten years ago, fifty years ago, two hundred years ago. Accordingly, our laws must change. And they do.

A broader point must be made. Since pre-school, teachers have been teaching you. They have decided that you must learn certain subject matter, and they have been devising ways to pour that subject matter into your brain and confirm that it got there. And you have submitted, acquiescing to the ministrations of the many teachers in your life. Law school will continue that process: your professors will hand you a syllabus, strut and fret before the assembled class in the lecture hall (or before the camera, if the lecture will be viewed online or later), and then they will make you take a final exam or write a term paper or the like. But one day, Dear Reader, a client will ask you a question, and *you will not know the answer*.

You could say, "I don't know," or "I don't practice in that area of the law," which are very acceptable answers sometimes. But you could know a lot more than the client about the body of knowledge surrounding the question, and still not know the answer. So you must **teach yourself** the answer, and then teach the client.

Fear not, Dear Reader! Getting tough questions, looking up the answers, devising solutions, and *helping clients* makes the practice of law so very rewarding! If you get nothing else from law school, endeavor to develop a system for teaching yourself stuff you do not already know. **Learn how to use the resources that reveal the law to you.**

Back in my day [insert geezer cough here], The Law came in the form of a Wall of Books. Court reporters, as they were called, contained all the case decisions for a certain jurisdiction. Index books allowed one to look up a keyword, for example, and find many of the cases that mentioned that keyword. Also, one could search a citation index to see other cases that cited a particular case. To capture fifty years of decisions, floor-to-ceiling bookshelves were needed. Research required the intrepid student to crawl (systematically!) through those books to get a thorough view of the law on a particular question.

Today, legal research is all done on computers. Computers save lots of the physical labor, and some of the mental labor, of legal research. Still, you need to know how to do legal research to serve as an attorney. It is as essential to an attorney as driving is to a taxi driver (umm, Uber® or Lyft® driver – sorry).

Let me tell you how I research the law. Depending on the question, sometimes I start with a Google® internet search. Yes, I look it up on the interwebs. I am looking for articles, blog entries by other attorneys, anything that can give me a high level view of the law. I take what I find with a grain of salt, for as Abraham Lincoln famously said, "Don't believe everything you see on the Internet." (He didn't really say that.)   Then I look for more "official" guidance – for example, the United States Patent and

Trademark Office ("USPTO") puts out a "Manual of Patent Examining Procedure" and a "Trademark Manual of Examining Procedure," both of which are available online. (I do intellectual property law.) Then, I will dive into the rules and the statutes that are mentioned in my reading. Those are often found on the USPTO website. Cases are found on Fastcase®, Lexis Nexis®, or Westlaw® online subscription services. Important: I go to **the source** of the law before I decide I am finished my legal research.

One key indicator of a successful and thorough legal research project: you know you are close to being done when several search strategies on several different platforms reveal the same results. You see references to the same cases, for example. Employ different keywords, strategies, and platforms to ensure that you have covered all of your bases.

Another goal of your research: You must find the most-authoritative case on a subject, and the most-recent case on that subject. So, you need to find that ten-year-old Supreme Court case that articulates the law, and you need to find the absolutely most-recent application of that law. Fill that in with a few cases over that ten-year span, and you have a pretty good idea of the law. Fail to get the latest case, and you could be writing about old law. What if the Supreme Court put out a decision yesterday that says, "Oops, we made a mistake ten years ago?"

Now that you know the law, how do you write about it?

B. Format and Style

What does a lawyer sound like? "Heretofore, one may have considered that a duly-licensed and recognized practicing attorney-at-law, accustom to all the rights and privileges appurtenant thereunto, should elaborate the represented party's legal positions and lawful rights with the most elegant and upright elocution." No. Let me dissuade you, Dear Reader, from busting out those fifty-cent words. (Except for "promulgate" – you can use that word.)

Attempting to speak with a fancy vocabulary will only *hinder* your ability to communicate. And *that* will impress no-one.

Instead, do two things. First, speak and write in **plain English**. Remember your audience includes clients, judges, fellow attorneys, jury members, and even the general public. They need to *understand* you. Let them be impressed with your clear style, comprehensive knowledge of the facts, and command of the law rather than your big long words. By "plain English," though, I do mean proper English. Follow grammatical rules, and run a spell-checker before you file that brief or term paper. I don't mean British English, unless of course you practice in Britain or elsewhere where they speak that dialect. If you need a good grammar book, I strongly recommend Ed Good's excellent and very funny treatment: C. Edward Good, *A Grammar Book for You and I ... Oops, Me!: All the Grammar You Need to Succeed in Life* (Capital Books, Inc. 2002).

Second, aim to communicate with **precision**. Say exactly what you mean, and nothing more, nothing less. Use the same word to indicate one and only one thing, and then use that word only to mention that one thing.

If you use proper grammar and communicate with precision, you will go far in the practice of law.

Let me throw in a bonus Thing You Can Do To Help You Communicate Like A Great Attorney: write with **action verbs**. "The book is on the table." Weak. Yes, it conveys a fact with precision. But how about: "The book stands on the table." "The book rests on the table." "The book stared accusingly from the table." Wow. You see the book come alive! The difference? The first sentence was written in passive voice, relying on the verb "to be," in the form "is." The other sentences speak in active voice, relying on action verbs, to stand, to rest, to stare. (Notice how the last two sentences juxtapose passive and active voice? Compare "was written" with "speak.") When you complete the first draft of any writing task, go through and circle all of the uses of the verb "to be." Then see if you can replace at least some of those uses with action verbs. For an elaboration of this and other fine tips, please read another of Ed Good's excellent books, C. Edward Good, *Mightier Than the Sword: Powerful Writing in the Legal Profession* (Word Store, 1989).

C. Citations

The practice of law, you will soon learn, is all about rules. You have Rules of Law. You have rules of procedure. You have rules of evidence. And you have rules of citation. Just follow the rules, Dear Reader, and you will do well.

The rules of citation govern how to cite a statute, regulation, case, treaty, article, web page, and the like – *anything*. Often, your Legal Research and Writing professor will pick a system of rules, and insist that you stick to that system. (Then, after law school, you will realize that not everyone uses that system! The horror!) Figure out which system your venue uses, and stick to that system! If your venue is a particular court, perhaps the rules of the court will tell you which system to use. Or call the clerk of court – they are very helpful. If your venue is your Legal Research and Writing course, ask your professor – they are very helpful, too.

The most widely-used system is set forth in *The Bluebook: A Uniform System of Citation* (Columbia Law Review Ass'n et al. eds., 20th ed. 2015). Dive into that resource and learn how to use it. Let me elaborate.

In your writing, you will want to cite to authority. I can tell you that a person must come to a complete stop at all stop signs before proceeding. You all know that, so I am not telling you anything you do not already know. It is more useful and powerful, however, to tell you that all drivers of vehicles must bring their vehicles to a complete stop at all stop signs before proceeding past that stop sign, and then cite the statute that says so. *See* S.C. Code Ann. § 56-5-2330(b) (2006). Further, in certain contexts it can be essential to recite the very statute itself:

Except when directed to proceed by a police officer, every driver of a vehicle approaching a stop sign shall stop at a clearly marked stop line but, if none, before entering the crosswalk on the near side of the intersection or, if none, then at the point nearest the intersecting roadway where the driver has a view of approaching traffic on the intersecting roadway before entering it. After having stopped, the driver shall yield the right-of-way to any vehicle in the intersection or approaching on another roadway so closely as to constitute an immediate hazard during the time when such driver is moving across or within the intersection or junction of roadways.

S.C. Code Ann. § 56-5-2330(b) (2006).

I hope the foregoing illustrates at least two things. First, increasing reliance upon the Rule of Law itself imparts greater accuracy and authority to your writing. My paraphrasing of the law suddenly looks sloppy once you read the actual words of the statute, doesn't it? Second, the hair on the back of your neck should stand up as you realize that you probably violate the stop sign law every time you roll halfway into the crosswalk before actually stopping. Yeah, that's the Power Of The Law, Dear Reader! It can make you a better driver! The larger point, of course, is that when you actually look up the law, great clarity and power come to you.

Notice how I cite that authority. My citation must direct you, Dear Reader, to the exact recitation of the law upon which I rely, so you can look it up, too. If I merely paraphrase the law, did I get it right? Did I omit anything relevant, like the police-officer-told-me-to-go exception? Did I mislead you in my paraphrase? Also, the year "(2006)" tells you the version of the law that I am citing. Perhaps a more-recent version of the statute controls. Importantly, the rules of citation set forth in *The Bluebook* and elsewhere standardize the citation of the law for two purposes or with two effects, at least. First, the reader can look up the law based on your citation.

Second, if you follow the citation rules, you subtly communicate to other attorneys including judges that you are an attorney, too. You signal that *I am a member of your club.* Indeed, "I am really good at employing the rules of citation," you say. "Beware, therefore: I am also really good at employing the Rules of Law in my client's favor."

Endeavor, therefore, to learn the rules of citation and employ them deftly in every legal work you write.

If you remain in doubt, there exists several online resources. LegalBluebook.com provides subscription access to the real deal. A few automatic citation generators also appear on the web, such as CitationMachine.net. Try them out and see if you can stump them! (Who said Legal Research and Writing was no fun?)

When you have completed your magnum opus of legal writing, look at every citation in your text, and double check it against your chosen (imposed) citation style guide. This is called "flyspecking." You are looking for the littlest specks of fly poop in your document and removing them. It is that thoroughness and diligence that marks a good attorney.

D. All Elements Rule

Now that you have the law, and know how to cite it, how do you write about it? The All Elements Rule should (soon) flow through your veins and brains, Dear Reader. You must address each and every element of the Rules of Law that you encounter. Once you write down the Rule of Law and all of its elements, then apply the law to the facts to determine whether each and every element is met in the circumstances. In actuality, "applying the law to the facts" means applying all of the relevant evidence relating to the first element, and then applying all of the relevant evidence to the second element, and so on, until all elements have been examined. If all elements are met, then the Rule of Law applies. If one element is missing, then the Rule does not apply.

E. All Evidence Suggestion

Your examination of the Rule of Law should employ all relevant facts and evidence. At some point early in your assessment of the legal conclusion you will reach, your process should liken to the placing of evidence on the scales of justice: all of the evidence in favor of one conclusion goes on one side of the scales, and all of the evidence in favor of the opposite conclusion goes on the other side of the scales. Then look and see which side is heavier – which side has the weightier evidence?

That is all well and good, and that is what judges and parents of quarreling toddlers (should) do all the time. But what if your client needs the Scales of Justice to tip in her favor? Or, what if your Legal Research and Writing professor wants you to advocate for a certain position? You must deal with "bad facts" that go against your desired conclusion. Do not ignore the evidence that weighs against you, but explain why they are less weighty, or do not add up. Is the witness not credible, because of bias? Is the evidence tainted because of a procedural violation or a failure in the chain of custody? Emphasize the evidence in your favor, and carefully explain away the evidence against.

F. Putting It All Together

Here's a checklist for your legal research and writing:

Do thorough research: Start general; get specific; go to the source.
Write in plain English with precision using action verbs.
Consistently employ the rules of citation.
Confirm that you follow the All Elements Rule for every Rule of Law raised in your writing.
Confirm that you follow the All Evidence Suggestion, and explain away Bad Facts.

When you have done the foregoing, you will find that you have read your work product many, many times. That's a good thing. A careful writer may "never" finish a document, because there will always be something that she can improve. With time and practice, and guidance from your professor, however, you will learn when you can let your document go for the enjoyment and scrutiny of your audience.

VI. Trial Advocacy

A. A War Story – All Elements Rule

In my Trial Advocacy course, my partner and I had to prosecute a defendant accused of armed robbery for stealing a purse from a lady in an elevator. A good friend of mine served as my witness, posing as the poor lady who had her purse stolen. Retelling the made-up details of facing her assailant and surrendering her purse under threat of physical violence and even death made my witness tear up on the witness stand. Her personal, visceral reaction reminds me how impactful and life-changing the circumstances surrounding a non-lawyer's appearance in court can be, no matter the circumstances. Think about it. Most people go to court only when there are pretty extreme events – a crime, a divorce, a "tort" or injury to person or property so significant that it is necessary to redress that injury in court.

My partner's witness was a police officer who apprehended the suspect in possession of the stolen purse. That witness served as a police officer in real life, and probably drew upon too many personal experiences in addition to the fictional police report provided him for this exercise.

Our judge was an impressive guy. A colonel in the Air Force, he served as a military judge and as a judge advocate general (lawyer in the military). He recorded our mock trial in shorthand, and was able to repeat back to us exactly what we said and how we said it, lawyers and witnesses. Later, he corrected me on my questioning technique. If you repeat the testimony of your own witness, you must incorporate it into the next question; you cannot simply make a statement and then ask a question, he explained. So, you cannot say: "You saw him pointing the knife at you. Then what did you do?" You must say, "When you saw him pointing the knife at you, what did you do?" The colonel's shorthand was that good. He was able to record my exact words and ding me on them an hour later. (Recall my friend who could recite the exchange in lecture three months later. Maybe shorthand is a skill a trial attorney should master!)

My partner and I presented our case. My witness testified, then the police officer. We got all of our evidence in. Weak objections were easily overcome. And we rested our case. Before they presented their case, the defense moved to dismiss on the ground that we had not proven one of the elements in the charge of armed robbery. To my horror, our judge was inclined to *grant the motion!*

Looking right at me, the judge said, "Your witness did not testify that there was anything of value in her purse. The charge of armed robbery requires as one of its elements that something of *value* be taken under armed threat of physical violence. How do you answer the defense's motion?"

" . . . [I will not repeat the weak answer I gave, lest you, Dear Reader, lose faith in me. Let's just say my reply did not defeat the motion to dismiss.] . . . ," said I.

The judge continued. "Your witness," he said, looking at my partner, indicating the police officer, "offered *hearsay* testimony that the victim had $40 in her purse. ["Hearsay" testimony is not allowed in court.] There was no objection to the hearsay testimony." The judge shot a brief, stern look at our opponents, not inviting a late objection, but instead spreading the condemnation a little more evenly. "Accordingly, the element of value has been met. Motion dismissed. The defense will now present its case."

The defense then presented their case. We raised objections where we could, but it was a sound presentation. At the end, the judge gave the victory to us by just a smidge.

"Now I am going to tell you everything that you did wrong. I am not going to tell you what you did right, so you will hear, and not ignore, what I tell you about what you did wrong." The judge proceeded to make us all better trial attorneys, one by one.

Overall, I felt exhilarated and exhausted. The victory did not figure prominently in my sentiment; instead, it was successfully completing the exercise that exhilarated me. Besides, our judge did not make us feel very victorious anyway.

My mock trial experience, Dear Reader, is Just One Reason why I live by the All Elements Rule today. One teeny weeny element goes missing, and poof! Your case is lost! So please, please, *please* internalize the All Elements Rule and follow it in every piece of written work, essay exam, memorandum of law, term paper, court brief, hearing, mock trial, trial, appellate hearing, and e-mail you ever write. (You will write a lot more e-mail messages than briefs, I bet!)

B. Another War Story – A Procedural Win Is A Win on the Merits!

The year before I attended law school, I was working as a "technical specialist" in a patent law firm in downtown Washington, D.C. In my spare time, and I had some spare time before starting law school, I would volunteer at the Our Lady of the Sacred Heart School for Adults, teaching people how to read. One day I was returning from teaching through a neighborhood where a good number of immigrants lived. On this summer evening, something was afoot. Four cop cars had lights flashing blue and red, and a number of young men were lined up against a wall, hands to the wall, legs spread. A team of police officers was in the process of arresting the young men.

The neighborhood buzzed with excitement as residents swarmed about, watching the police arrest the young men. Importantly, people walked every which way, including into the street, completely ignoring all customs and laws about walking on sidewalks and crossing the street at intersections. And they craned their necks to watch the police arresting the young men, seemingly oblivious to the vehicular traffic, of which I was a part, crawling through the excited crowd. It seemed to me that the neighborhood was on the brink of rioting. I became very eager to gently push my car through the swarming crowd and get out of there as quickly and as safely as I could.

I noticed in my rearview mirror one of the four cop cars leaving the scene to travel down the street behind me. At that moment, amid the swarming people moving this way and that, a woman and her young daughter stood perfectly still, just off the curb in the crosswalk I was cruising though. The blue and red lights came on, and I got to meet one of D.C.'s Finest – a no-nonsense lady with a pony tail who did not give a darn where I had just been or what volunteer work I had been doing.

I got a lot of tickets that day – I couldn't find my registration; my inspection sticker had expired; and maybe there was one other administrative violation thrown in. Germane to our story, the big ticket was for failing to yield to a pedestrian in a crosswalk. And it was a doozy.

Well, I did as any self-respecting fresh-faced new employee of a big law firm in Washington, D.C., would do. I was going to fight it! I did my research, and I even asked for discovery – I wanted to show from police reports that a major event (the arrests) was underway, and the neighborhood was nearly rioting when I allegedly failed to yield to a pedestrian in a crosswalk. I would tell the court that rather than get entangled in the near-riot – after volunteer-teaching at Our Lady of the Sacred Heart School for Adults, I will have you know – I chose to proceed as reasonably and safely as I could. (I have no idea if any of that would have done anything to get me out of the ticket, but I had to try something.)

My day in court – to try the failure-to-yield ticket – came. I had all of my evidence in a three-ring binder, and I was ready. Well, as ready as any non-attorney could be. Know that I had not even taken Trial Advocacy yet, but I was a second-year law student in one of the finest law schools in the land, darn it! So I strode into the courtroom and was prepared to wait for my case to be called. Significantly, I had not received my requested discovery – the police reports – and the judge was going to hear all about it. Still, I was nervous, and did not know what to expect at all.

The courtroom was busy. This was traffic court, and everybody and their grandmother were there, waiting to try their cases. In D.C. traffic court, there was no pleading out to get a reduced sentence. You either paid the ticket as written, or you faced a full trial. Also, there was no "pro se" representation to speak of; that is, the court strongly encouraged each defendant to retain an attorney. A group of public defenders hung out in the back, waiting to be assigned to a case when the judge determined that a defendant was indigent enough. The threshold for indigency did not seem high, and the public defenders kept busy.

In the back of the courtroom, one of the public defenders noticed my, ahem, "deer-in-the-headlights" look, and asked me what I had. He was a grizzled man in a rumpled suit, towering over me, the smell of cheap drugstore-brand mouthwash occasionally wafting over me. I told him the whole story as briefly as I could, showing my binder as a youngster might show his artwork to a parent. His kind eyes barely hid his lawyerly calculations as he listened to my strategery.

"Okay, here's what you do, kid." He said animatedly, once I had finished. (I am pretty sure he called me "kid.") "When the judge asks if you are ready for trial, do not answer. If you say, 'yes,' then the prosecutor can ask for a continuance [a delay in trial to another day]. Instead, look over at the prosecutor. It's his job to be ready. If he is not, then you move to dismiss. Got it, kid?"

"Yes, sir! Thank you, sir!" My nervousness softened a notch with his seasoned advice. I closed my binder and resumed my waiting. Soon my case was called. I was about to try my first case!

The judge, a white-haired man in a black robe, asked me where was my attorney. I explained that I had been given permission to represent myself at my arraignment, since I was a law student. He glanced down at the file in front of him, and I presume he assessed that the case was small potatoes all things considered, and allowed me to proceed.

"Are you ready for trial?" the judge asked, looking right at me. Slowly, deliberately, I turned my head to look right at the prosecutor, hoping the judge's gaze followed mine. The prosecutor, himself a young man not much older than I, stood up. "Your Honor, as an officer of the court, it is my duty to inform the court that the People are not ready to proceed with this case," he stated for the record.

The judge's white-haired head swiveled back to me. "I move to dismiss?" I stammered, my voice cracking a little on the last word. The judge nodded, encouragingly, as if to say, "Yes, kid! That's *exactly* what you are supposed to say!" And that is how I won my first trial.

The take-home message, Dear Reader, is that a win on procedural grounds is a win on the merits. You might decide that I was truly guilty of failing to yield to a pedestrian on the merits, but the prosecutor had not followed proper procedure. He had not given me the discovery he owed me. Accordingly, I won on a procedural ground. The law has all kinds of rules, as I have mentioned: substantive Rules of Law, procedural rules, rules of evidence, and citation rules found in *The Bluebook.* You have to follow them all. Yes, all those systems of rules seem complicated. But then so did chess seem complicated when you had mastered only checkers. Or driving a car when all you knew was bicycles. Study and apply all those rules, and do it better than your opponent, and you will do extremely well in the practice of law.

So how do you try a case in a mock trial?

C. Offense

In every mock trial fact pattern, there will be something affirmative for you to prove, and something for you to disprove or prevent your opponent from proving. For example, if you are the prosecutor, you will have to prove that the defendant did the crime charged. You will also have to disprove, or prevent the defense from proving, something: an alibi, or often an affirmative defense, for example. "I shot the guy, but in self-defense," is a defense you probably know. Or, sometimes the defense will charge the plaintiff with a counterclaim. A counterclaim is a cause of action that says your client owes the other side money. A counterclaim puts the plaintiff on defense. Indeed, the plaintiff is called "the counterclaim defendant." So let us break your case into "offense," meaning the claim you have to prove, and "defense," meaning the claim or other matter your opponent has to prove. You will have a plan for offense and a plan for defense, no matter whether you are plaintiff or prosecutor, on one hand, or defendant on the other.

So let's look at your offensive strategy. Do I need to mention the **All Elements Rule**? Carefully assess the Rule of Law governing your offensive case, and look hard at each and every element. Make a list of those elements, and then line up all of the evidence that supports each of those elements. What evidence makes it more likely than not that a given element is met? What is the most compelling evidence to support a given element? What is the direct evidence? What is the circumstantial evidence? Do you have enough evidence to meet the burden of proof, such as "a preponderance of the evidence" in a civil trial, or "beyond a reasonable doubt" in a criminal trial?

Once you have identified the evidence supporting a given element, plan how you are going to get that evidence "admitted into evidence." Admission into evidence means that you have presented that evidence in a manner that complies with all the rules of evidence. For example, testimony from the owner of the purse that her purse contained $40 would be properly admitted; testimony from the police officer that the victim said she had $40 in her purse would not be admitted, because it is hearsay evidence: the cop did not personally know whether the purse had $40 in it, but that testimony would be offered to prove that the purse in fact held $40.

Look at every single piece of evidence, and plan more than one way to get it in. Do not assume that one way will get it in easily. A witness may forget, or not show up to court. Plan for the various contingencies, and be ready to overcome foreseeable objections.

To prepare for trial, write out a script of questions and answers for each of your witnesses. Do NOT show this script to your witnesses, so you cannot be accused of coaching your witness. But this script should guide you to ask all the questions to elicit all of the testimony you need. Moreover, this script will help you remember to introduce the evidence you need (and *how* to introduce that evidence). Importantly, your script should include contingencies such as for refreshing the witnesses' memories, of course conducted in accordance with the rules of evidence.

In real life trials, we prepare "witness books," binders that contain every exhibit (document) a given witness will need, and a few extra exhibits that we might not use unless the witness forgets or another issue comes up. The script ties the exhibits to the questions, and ensures that you will remember the right questions to ask to establish the foundation for each exhibit. An exhibit book for each of your witnesses will be a useful tool for you, especially if there is lots of evidence to organize.

Also plan or prepare your demonstrative exhibits. Demonstratives are not "real evidence," but they summarize or explain real evidence. Charts and graphs, prepared beforehand or as testimony unfolds, can assist the trier of fact to understand your case. For example, a large photograph of the crime scene can illustrate what happened, as the witness marks up the photograph during her testimony. The marked-up photograph becomes a demonstrative exhibit separate from the photograph itself. (Get both versions of the photograph admitted!)

Iteratively, repeatedly, consult the rules of evidence and the rules of procedure (and any applicable court rules) that will govern your trial. Like the All Evidence Rule, those systems of rules cause your case to live or die. When can you ask witnesses about habits, reputations, or prior convictions? How do you lay a foundation for a photograph?

Finally, prepare your opening and closing statements. Essentially, you will tell a story of what happened, and the legal significance of that story. Match your story to your case. If your client has an alibi, then your story is "she didn't do it." But if your defense rests on a missing element, then "she didn't do it" is not your story. "The prosecution cannot prove it" forms your thesis there. Write out and practice your opening and closing several times to make them go as smoothly as possible. Avoid trying to recite them from memory; rather, practice them so many times that you can tell the story because you have *internalized* that story. Of course, your story should touch on all elements of the Rule of Law that you have to prove. But here's where you tell a story more than you merely check off a list of elements.

Then when you are finished planning your offence, do two things. First, double check against the All Elements Rule. Have you forgotten any elements? What about subparts of elements, or that three-prong test to prove the fourth element? Second, anticipate how your opponent will fight your offensive case. Go back and line up all the evidence *against* each element. Consider how you will explain away, or better yet, prevent "bad" evidence from ever getting admitted into evidence in the first place. Remember, a procedural win is a win on the merits! Make certain that you do not ignore bad facts! If your opponent dwells on them and you have no rebuttal, you do your case and client a major disservice.

D. Defense

Now it is time to prepare your defense. Your opponent has something to prove. Imagine that *you* have to prove it. How would you do that? What evidence lines up in favor of each element your opponent has to prove? Are there any evidentiary difficulties in proving any of the elements? Examining this will help you spot vulnerabilities in your opponent's case.

Look for ways to exclude evidence and to counter or explain those bad facts that support your opponent's claims. Plan your objections, and how you will counter foreseeable rebuttals.

Write a script for cross-examining your opponent's witnesses. Challenge credibility where you cannot exclude evidence. Is the only neutral eyewitness to whether the traffic light was green or red actually suffering from poor vision or distracted attention? Prepare your own witness books for cross examination, if the body of evidence is extensive. Importantly, plan how you are going to use each piece of evidence, and whether and how you are going to get your rebuttal evidence admitted.

Plan out your exhibits as well. Sometimes, the exhibits you use will be the same exhibits your opponent uses. For consistency, be prepared to elicit testimony on cross examination from the same exhibit the witness used on direct examination. That way, the transcript will refer to, for example, "Defense Exhibit 5" the whole way through. But be careful: your opponent might use a different exhibit than one that tells your story. For example, a cropped photograph might hide an important detail, such as the bushes that obscured the view of a witness. So have your own versions of the exhibits ready where foreseeably necessary.

E. Final Preparation

The day before your trial, take the time to re-read every bit of evidence. Read all of the documents, deposition transcripts, and demonstrative exhibits. That exercise will give you the best recall of the details that make up the case. Seriously, your mind will swim with the facts and evidence that support your case. But unless you re-read everything, details will escape you. Your opponent may assert facts that are not supported by the evidence. You cannot foresee your opponent's spin, but you can re-familiarize yourself with the entire body of evidence so that you can spot a bad spin when it happens.

Make sure your exhibits are ready, and think through the mechanics of your presentation. Will you need to have a flipchart handy? Will you ask your witness to come off the stand to demonstrate how she grappled with her assailant?

Confirm that your witnesses are prepared, and that they know when and where to go. The raw mechanics of showing up on time and prepared carry a disproportionate weight on the success or failure of many a proceeding. Have your witnesses re-read their materials thoroughly, so their memories are refreshed.

Do a quick review of the law. What are the elements of your Rule of Law? What are the elements of any affirmative defense or counterclaim that your opponent must prove? Look through the rules of evidence and the rules of procedure that will govern your trial.

Finally, take a deep breath. Doing a trial can be a lot of fun, so try to enjoy yourself. It will get easier with practice!

F. Checklist for Trial Preparation

Here, I have boiled down the foregoing into a neat little checklist for easy reference:

Prepare your offense:
Determine all elements of your claim.
Line up each piece of evidence tending to prove each element.
Plan how to enter each of those pieces into evidence.
Address "bad facts."
Prepare script of questions, answers, and exhibits for each witness.
Prepare witness books.
Plan demonstrative exhibits.
Double check rules of evidence and procedure, and the elements of your claim.
Prepare opening and closing statements.

Prepare your defense:
Determine all elements of your opponent's claim.

Line up each piece of evidence tending to prove each element.

Determine how to block or explain each piece of evidence.

Plan your objections.

Write a script for cross-examining opponent's witnesses.

Prepare exhibit books for cross examination.

Final Preparation:

Re-read everything.

Confirm your witnesses are prepared and know when and where to show up.

Review the law.

Relax and enjoy!

VII. Extracurriculars

A. The Rock Star Career

If no-one ever told you, the absolute pinnacle of law school success upholds the chair of the senior editor of your law school's law review. Only the most-accomplished, wicked-smart law student gets to sit in that chair. Why, it seems pre-ordained that if you serve as the senior editor of your law school review, you will later serve as a Supreme Court justice or the attorney general of the United States.

What is a "law review" anyway? The law review is a journal or magazine that publishes scholarly articles about the law. The student editors put the editions of the law review together, and gather to fight over proper *Bluebook* citation in those articles. Student editors also solicit articles to fill the law review. Sometimes those articles come from practicing lawyers or even judges. Also, many articles are "student notes," written by the editors, perhaps, or by enterprising students who want a good writing sample for later job-seeking use. A law review can enshrine the latest and greatest scholarship produced by a law school, and act as a monument for the ages to the legal thinking happening at your law school. Accordingly, being named senior editor carries profound prestige.

Okay, great. The smartest smarty-pants in the school gets to be the senior editor. What about the rest of us poor slobs? What do we get for our tuition?

B. And For the Rest of Us?

Law schools offer many wonderful extra-curricular activities beyond simply *Bluebooking* other people's law review articles. In addition to the other positions on the law review, you can seek out participation on the mock trial team, the mediation board, and other "mock" practice clubs. Also, there can be more than one law review, such as law reviews dedicated to a special area of the law like environmental law or international law.

At the end of your first year of law school, every first-year student will be invited to apply to each of the several extracurricular organizations. The application may require a writing sample, or participation in a competition. For example, the mock trial team may require you to deliver an opening statement based on a hypothetical case. The mediation board may require a mock negotiation. For the uber-prestigious law review, your first-year grades also come into play. Membership is determined by upperclassmen who are already members of those organizations. I hate to say it, but there may be politics involved, since upperclassmen are people, too. It would not hurt your chances to befriend a member or two of the law review. Membership decisions may be announced before you finish your second semester, or at the start of your third semester so your grades can be considered.

C. Practical Experience

Sure, editing articles, arguing mock trials, and negotiating fake deals impart experience to a student. However, there is a certain let's-play-lawyer aspect to that experience, because the outcomes impact no-one. Increasingly, law schools also provide real-world experience through pro bono clinics. "Pro bono" means "for the good," and practically means, "free legal services" for those who become clients. Law schools endeavor to provide clinical experience for their students, at least in part to help them obtain employment as lawyers after law school. Clinics, overseen by professors and sometimes practicing lawyers, allow law students to provide legal services to the community in real cases. How exciting is that! You get to serve real people with real legal problems long before you graduate from law school.

I strongly urge you, Dear Reader, to explore ways to obtain real-world experience while in law school. That could mean getting a job in a law firm. Or it could mean serving in a pro bono clinic sponsored by your law school. Some law schools specialize in providing clinics focusing on a certain area of the law, such as criminal defense for minor crimes, landlord-tenant law, family law, and the like. Seek out the clinical experience you desire, especially if you think you might like to practice in a certain area of the law.

D. Fun for Everyone!

At the end of the day, law school should be fun. Learning the law in lectures involves a certain kind of stimulation that can be fun. Another kind of law school fun inhabits your extracurricular activities. Enjoy!

Your extracurricular activities also teach you another skill that cannot be learned elsewhere. That skill relates to dealing with opposing counsel. If you win your cases in real life, your clients love you and you get paid. If you lose, well, things ain't so rosy. And there is a team of Really Smart Persons on the other side of the courtroom working *hard* to make you lose. They are opposing counsel. With experience, you will learn to be magnanimous in victory and gracious in defeat toward your opposing counsel. But in your first trial, you may find you hate their guts! Practice seeing your opposing counsel as a fellow professional, just trying to do the best job for each client as you do. You will win some, and you will lose some. Some victories you will deserve, and others, not so much. Same goes for defeats. You will feel far better about a defeat if your well-prepared opponent performed very well and *earned* the win. Make them earn it, and you earn your wins, too. Remember what you learned from your tee-ball coach: overall, it is not about whether you win or lose, but how you play the game!

VIII. Gaining Job Experience

A. The Rock Star Career, Continued

Where does the senior editor of the law review go after law school? If she really wants that rock star career, she gets a clerkship on a federal appellate court for a year. And, if she really shines there, she gets invited to a clerkship on the United States Supreme Court. Yes, that is how it happens. So how do you line up that career as a law student? Earn top grades, write a fabulous article to serve as your writing sample, get on law review and earn the senior editor spot, and then get a series of powerful clerkships, and you, too, can clerk for a justice on the Supreme Court.

Then what? The Rock Star Career might land you in a prestigious law firm specializing in appellate work for a few years. Then you might serve as a professor at one of the best law schools in the country while you wait for the call to serve on the Supreme Court or as an attorney general. If you want people virtually genuflecting as you walk by because you are God's gift to the law, then that's how you roll.

B. Clerkships and Internships

For the rest of us, who are not God's (greatest) gift to the law, a clerkship on a court can launch a fabulous legal career nonetheless. That is true even if the court is your local county's family law court, especially if you want to practice family law when you become A Real Live Attorney.

A law clerk serves a judge by doing a lot of research and writing. Routinely, a law clerk will write memoranda for her judge, explaining the law as revealed by thorough research, and possibly applying the law to the facts of the case the judge is deciding. A judge might ask two of her law clerks to write opposing memoranda on a particular issue, or on the whole case Her Honor has to decide. So you have to know your legal research skills and resources very well. And you need to know how to write very well. But do not worry: there is also a lot of on-the-job training in the clerkship position, and you will get better at research, writing, and legal reasoning. Think of a clerkship as an apprenticeship. You are not supposed to have mastered the art of being a lawyer (or a judge!) just yet.

I am telling you this so you do not settle for a "C" in your Legal Research and Writing course, (and settle for "Cs" in your other courses) and declare that mediocrity is good enough. The skills and knowledge you learn in law school will serve you very well, both in landing that first job, perhaps a clerkship, and throughout your legal career.

Internships, as I use that term, are for law students, while clerkships are for recent law school graduates. I had a few friends that served judges as unpaid interns during law school. Because I worked for a law firm that practiced before the judge who taught my patent law course, I decided the conflict of interests might be too complicated, so I did not seek out internship opportunities. How could I serve as an intern to a judge deciding a case for which my employer advocated one side?

You need three things to apply for an internship or a clerkship. First, you need grades. Your grades do not need to be at the very top of your class, but they should be respectable. Second, you need a writing sample. Students with foresight work hard in their Legal Research and Writing course to pen a document that they can use as a writing sample. That saves them the effort of having to write a second document. Third, you need one or more letters of recommendation. Befriend, or at least do not routinely insult, your professors, clinic advisors, and employers. You may need to ask them the favor of writing you a letter of recommendation so that you can get to that next opportunity.

C. Summer Associate Programs in Big Law

If a lawyer ever enjoys a fairy-tale existence, it is during the summer before the final year of law school. If her grades are high, she could land a position at a large law firm as a "summer associate." Her days will fill with interesting softball tasks, while her evenings and weekends will fill with socializing and adventures ranging from visits to the local courthouse to white water rafting. (I am serious about the white water rafting!) A law firm hires a cohort of summer associates to woo them to join the firm as associates after law school. Accordingly, the law firm puts its best foot forward, and every lawyer knows to be on her best behavior in the presence of the summer associates. It really is a fun time for all.

I served as a "student associate" in a big law firm, and got to see the magnificent and cushy life of a summer associate. Often, I was invited to participate in those wonderful events, too, because the law firm was wooing me to remain as an associate after law school. (Often I had to decline participation in the excursions because I had work to do!)

Summer associates at my firm enjoyed two incredible benefits on top of the constant fete-ing and kid-glove work assignments. First, they were paid about what they would make as a new attorney.

In a big law firm, that pay will make your eyes pop out. Second, at the end of the summer, nearly all summer associates would receive job offers to return as associates once law school finished. Now, Dear Reader, I believe *your* eyes are popping out. (I will pause while you pop them back in.) So yes, it is A Very Good Thing to land a summer associate position in a big law firm.

Know that *associate* attorneys work hard to pay for your *summer associate* experience. And you will have to take a turn on that oar when you become an associate in that big law firm.

To land a summer associate position, you need good grades, a writing sample, and a letter of recommendation or two. If Big Law is your thing, contact the human resources department at the firms that interest you to find out how to apply.

D. Law Clerks in Law Firms

Many law firms also offer "law clerk" positions to full-time law students, and "student associate" positions to part-time (evening) law students. These positions employ the law students during the academic year, and distinguish from the summer associate position. Law clerk positions also can be had by law school graduates who have not passed the bar exam. Law clerks work hard for low pay, and life sucks compared to the life enjoyed by summer associates. But that stems from the fact that law clerks actually work! Clerking in a law firm provides a great way to really put your finger on the pulse of the firm. What a great thing to do before you commit as an associate attorney after law school.

E. Legal Clinics

As stated in the previous chapter, legal clinics sponsored by your law school can impart useful (critical?) real-world experience. That experience can help you land a job after law school, because it can show your potential employer that you actually can do legal work with real-world consequences. You will have hands-on skills and experience, and that should impress any would-be employer.

IX. Evening Law School!

A. Advantages

I loved law school more than any other educational experience over all – comparing college, graduate school, and law school. And *evening* law school made it even better. I enjoyed several advantages by attending evening law school. First of all, I was able to work while attending law school. That allowed me to pay for much of law school without taking out more loans. Once you graduate, many more options will be available to you if you owe a smaller mountain of student loan debt. Those options range from job opportunities to home purchases.

Second, the pace of law school was a little slower. I had two or three finals at the end of each semester, instead of three, four, or five. A related aspect of this, I could pick courses based on the final exam schedule. I endeavored to space out my final exams as much as possible. I am certain that I performed better on each final exam with two or three days between them than I would have if the exams were on the same day or sequential days.

Third, I was able to gain work experience in a law firm while many of my classmates could not. Real world work experience is becoming more important for newly-minted attorneys seeking jobs. Now, as the managing member of my own law firm, I feel it from the other side: a fine academic record looks great, but can the attorney job candidate actually do the work?

B. A Day in the Life of Jeremy

Here's how my day went, while attending evening law school. I would get up about 7:00 AM, exercise, do my daily ablutions, and go to work. I lived near the Foggy Bottom Metro Station in Washington, D.C., and the law firm where I worked was located just two Metro stops away at McPherson Square Metro Station. (It was extraordinarily important to me that I lived close to work and school, as time was so precious.) I'd eat breakfast and lunch at work, and while there, work, work, work. Just before 5 PM, I would head home. I would have a snack and possibly a power nap (yeah!). Then I would review very briefly the reading for that evening's lecture, and at 5:45 PM, I would leave for the four-block walk to The George Washington University Law School lecture hall. After lecture finished at 8 PM, I would walk home, eat dinner, and do the reading for the next day's lecture. I would annotate the cases as described above. Sometimes I would even practice what I would say if I were called on to brief a case. Practicing the words allowed me to respond more smoothly when the Unthinkable (*Inevitable*) happened. I was in bed by 11 PM.

On the weekends, I would read at least for Monday's lecture, work on long-term projects like term papers, and do all those other things besides work and school that one must do when prosecuting life on this planet. Nonetheless, I have to admit, I greatly curtailed my social life while in law school – I finally decided that I could not really date while there. Working and going to law school was so intense that I really had nothing much to say in the way of light conversation. "So, um, we are learning about negligence in law school, and this funny case held that a traffic ticket could make you liable for neg – hey, wait! Where are you going? Don't you want to finish your drink?" Yeah, I wasn't much fun. Unlike now. I'm this really fun guy who writes about law sch – hey, wait, Dear Reader! Where are you going? Don't you want to finish this chapter?

I digress.

C. The Important Stuff

Whether you attend day or evening law school, it is important that you maintain your health and sanity. Stay in touch with your family, your friends, your roots. The intensity of law school, and the transformative nature of the education, impose serious risks to your existing relationships if you are not fiercely diligent in nurturing them. Unfortunately, law school students get divorced at a higher rate per capita than the general public. That is because law school demands so much from you, and has the power to change you. Use that change to better, deepen, and strengthen your relationships. But it is powerful stuff.

What can you do? Do those things that everyone else has to do – date nights with your beloved, weekend trips to the zoo with the kids: *cultivate* those relationships so they will be there when you finish. And try, try, *try hard* not to talk about the latest legal doctrines you are learning *all the time*. A million-dollar question that you can use in so many contexts: **"And you?"** Ask your spouse how she is doing, and pay attention. Try not to outline an essay answer in reaction to the fact pattern that was her day.

Finally, pray. Pray for the strength, wisdom, and stamina to endure the marathon that is law school. You can do it; a little Grace From Above can help!

X. Paying for Law School

Back in my day [cough, cough, cough], I estimated that my law school education cost $75,000 over four years. Overall, my education cost about $150,000, and I went to *Grade 24*. Those numbers pale in comparison to the mountainous costs today's law school students face. Tuition alone easily tops $60,000/year at many private law schools. In-state tuition at public law schools runs about half that. Living expenses, books, and supplies add about $20,000/year. So you really have to want to go to law school before taking that plunge. How do people do it?

A. Work For It

Obviously, one very good way to pay for some or all of law school is to work. Gone are the days where a person could work at a relatively low-paying job, like in a coffee shop, and earn enough money to live and pay for law school. No. Today, a person must work as a professional and pull down a good salary just to cover living expenses and have a little left over for tuition. Trouble is, work is *work*. After a full day of work, a person is exhausted. Now imagine heading off to lecture to face being called on. "Johnson! [Insert your name here.]" "Johnson! Wake up and tell us the holding in *Smith v. Jones*." Doesn't sound like much fun. But if you can defray at least some of the costs with your take-home pay, any debt you must take on will be smaller. And, sometimes, if you are super lucky, your employer will pay some or all of your tuition. But watch the fine print for those golden handcuffs, chaining you to that employer for years afterwards in exchange.

Here's a beautiful aspect of tuition. There may be ways to make it tax-deductible. Perhaps you can cycle it through a 529 plan. Perhaps you can write it off as an investment in your professional development. However, be very careful as you consider ways of lawfully avoiding paying taxes on your law school tuition and costs. Consult a qualified tax professional *before* you do *anything*. The risks are high: if you screw it up, your tax evasion conviction may bar you from ever serving as an attorney!

B. Uncle Sam Needs You

Another beautiful way to pay for law school is by serving your country in the armed forces, and then using the GI Bill benefits you earn to pay for law school. My Dad did this; many others have done so as well. Once you earn it, the GI Bill is a sweet deal. Spouses and kids of veterans also may qualify.

Friends who worked for the government sometimes scored tuition reimbursement. Patent examiners could have the federal government pay for law school tuition, but they owed time as attorneys afterward: the so-called "golden handcuffs." It was not a bad deal, but some cannot stand the indentured servitude of golden handcuffs. For others, golden handcuffs and a guaranteed job were better than the leaden ball and chain of massive debt and uncertain employment.

C. Borrow Like a Politician

If you have convinced yourself that law school must be conquered for you to advance in your chosen Life Plan, then go for it! Many professionals take on significant debt as an investment in their careers. All investments are bets. This one is a bet on yourself. How much do you believe in yourself? How badly do you want it?

Just know two things. First, you will have to pay it back – at least most of it. You can declare bankruptcy, but these loans will stick with you. So just take a deep breath and know that you will be making monthly payments for a long time unless and until you win the lottery. But not to worry. You can consolidate and restructure as needed to make the payments fit your budget, whatever it may be.

Second, your student loan debt may limit you. You may be forced to take a higher-paying job, for example. I know many a dreamer who focused on environmental law during law school because they wanted to save the world and abolish pollution. Upon graduation, however, they faced the prospect of having to work for the Dark Side (corporate America), looking for loopholes in the law to allow Darth Corporation to *keep* polluting. (Corporate America ain't so bad; and you should *never* do anything that goes against your principles or causes you to hate yourself!) You will be less able to borrow money for a house, for another example.

So what can you do? A few things:

First, borrow as little as possible. That means structuring your law school life as economically as you can. Attend that less-expensive law school, and live with Mom and Dad if you can. (Do you really want to borrow $45,000 to $60,000 over three years so you can live in a rocking party pad?) I have heard it said, "Live like a lawyer while you are a student, and you will live like a student when you are a lawyer!" Do not drink $5 lattes every day. Lawyers don't even do that – we can't afford them!

Second, apply for student aid. Grants and scholarships can be yours for the asking. But you have to ask. I know students who negotiated with two or more law schools, and attended the school with the best package. The packages can be significant! Because my employer at the time reimbursed law school tuition, I never asked. Once I learned about the packages others were getting from law schools, I felt foolish for not having inquired myself!

Third, seek the best deals on your student loans. Shop around. See if you can get federally-guaranteed loans and loans with deferred payments while you are in school. You do not want to borrow money to pay back borrowed money. And the lower the interest rates, the less interest you will have to pay in the long run. Frankly, I prefer federally-backed loans over loans from private banks, at least because there are loan balance forgiveness programs if you jump through lots of hoops. See the next section in this chapter.

Fourth, seek work during law school. Relevant work experience will help you land

126

a better job upon graduation; it will also help defray a little bit of the cost of attending law school or at least living expenses while you are in law school.

Fifth, commit to paying back your loans as soon as possible. I know it looks like an enormous task, and it is difficult to even conceive of an accelerated repayment plan when you don't know what your post-law school life will even look like. But here is one strategy: structure your loans for a low monthly payment, so your monthly budget will have the lightest burden possible. That way, if you have a lot of expenses one month, or God forbid, you have trouble getting a job, the pain of making that payment is lessened. Then, as part of that strategy, make extra principal payments every chance you get. Throw random amounts at the Loan Beast. Pay set amounts each month. Do whatever it takes to slay that beast sooner rather than later. Your middle age will be more pleasant without that debt repayment to worry about each month. When you make an extra payment on your principal, however, be sure to insist that your bank

"PAY PRINCIPAL NOW." I have heard of banks receiving an extra payment, and not crediting the payment against principal: the bank holds the extra payment for some future time so the bank makes the most interest possible.

Sixth, visit the U.S. Department of Education's websites (www.ed.gov and www.studentaid.ed.gov), and educate yourself about federal loan programs and repayment schemes. They have a comprehensive loan repayment calculator that estimates your repayment amounts in several repayment schemes. I punched in the following numbers just for fun: My hypothetical law school graduate is single and lands a job paying $60,000 per year. Our hero owes $100,000 on a federally-subsidized qualified loan at 4 % interest. Under the standard repayment plan, she would pay $1,012 per month for 120 months (ten years), for a total of $121,440. If she opted for an "extended, graduated" repayment plan in which her monthly payments would be significantly lower at first, rise over time, and take 300 months (twenty-five years), then she would pay

$333 to $945 per month for a total of $173,166. Ahh! You see that the privileges of lower monthly payments and a longer time to repay translate into $51,726 more interest – almost a year's salary dedicated to pay for those privileges. (Of course her pay will not be stuck at $60,000 per year forever.) That is why I am a huge fan of paying off debt as aggressively as you can. You can save on interest in a big way.

D. Student Loan Forgiveness Programs

Magically, some of those federal loan-repayment programs forgive any unpaid balances remaining at the end of the repayment period, be it twenty or twenty-five years. That's it! Poof! Gone! You don't owe a penny, if the loans are qualified and you faithfully made your payments. Well, ahem, there is one caveat: forgiven debt is taxable income, so don't get too excited about socking it to Uncle Sam. When you wash your hands of say $100,000 in student loan debt, you might owe on the order of $30,000 in taxes as if you had received that $100,000 in cash. Yikes.

Even more magic happens if you qualify for the Public Service Loan Forgiveness ("PSLF") program. After you make 120 qualifying monthly payments while working for a qualifying employer (usually a government agency), poof! Any student loan balance remaining disappears! In other words, your loan balance goes to zero after ten years if you are working for the public interest. It is a political football whether student debt forgiveness under the PSLF program is taxable, so do your homework before you set your heart on it.

More information about these programs appear at the U.S. Department of Education's websites, www.ed.gov and www.studentaid.ed.gov.

It would not be a horrible fate for a twenty-five-year-old law school graduate to commit to a ten-year stint as a public defender and/or prosecutor, and then launch a private practice once the student loans are repaid and forgiven. I know you have lots of plans and much to do in the ten years after law school, but hey, if you owe

$200,000, you have to figure out some way to handle that. Under the standard repayment plan, that would require you to cough up $2,024 per month for ten years. If you can get away with lower payments and then obtain forgiveness for the rest, it could be an excellent way to launch a legal career.

XI. Final Word of Encouragement – Find Your "Why"

Dear Reader, I hope this book has given you something useful. More than that, I hope this book helps you **thrive** in law school, so you enjoy it as much as I did. Remember to keep up with the reading on your syllabus, and practice answering essay test questions early and often. Indulge in some extracurricular activities, write an awesome paper that you can use as a writing sample, and gain some real-world experience in a legal clinic or job. And remember to enjoy it all!

Here (hereinabove), I have addressed a lot of the *how*. How do you study for a final exam, how do you prepare for a mock trial. But I urge you, Dear Reader, also to examine the **why**. Why are you going to law school? Why do you want to be an attorney? To make money? Sure. That is why I went to law school. I could not find a job as a chemist. But money will not sustain you, I respectfully submit. Once you land that big job and start making money, you will see that money really cannot buy you happiness. Consider how you felt upon graduating from high school. Elation? How long did that wonderful feeling last before you started worrying about college? Now you have graduated from college. By the end of June, you will ask yourself whether you can really hack law school. (**You can!**) When law school finishes, you will promptly begin worrying about the bar exam. (Not to worry! I have published two helpful books on the subject: *How to Pass the Bar Exam with Dr. Stipkala's Proven Method* (Persimmon Woods Press, LLC 2018), and *Perspectives on Passing the Bar Exam: How We Did It; and How You Can, Too!* (Persimmon Woods Press, LLC 2018)) And, one day, when you win that Big Case, you will promptly begin worrying (a) what about the next case? and (b) where will your next paycheck come from? My point: there is always something new to worry about, and money will not absolve you from worry. That is true even if you make a *pile* of money.

Your "why" must come from somewhere else – to sustain you through the tough times, the hard work, the setbacks and defeats. And your "why" must sustain you through the victories and the good times as well, lest you get carried away and are left unprepared for the tough times when they come. Dear Reader, consider my "why," and further consider adapting and adopting it as your own.

The hallmark of a satisfied attorney, in my considerable experience, is that she gets up every day to **help people**. This is true no matter your practice context. For example, it is easy to conjure mental images of indigents who need legal assistance, and then to picture yourself nobly serving the tired, poor, huddled masses. But corporations and government agencies also comprise people, and those people need their livelihoods protected and their missions advanced, all in accordance with the law. Resolve to serve your clients as you would serve yourself.

If you can develop your "why" as you build your own personal "how," you will lay a solid foundation for a satisfying career as an attorney-at-law. Moreover, a sound, sustainable "why" can guide you as make choices in your study and practice of the law. Endeavor to look out for the **client's best interest** every time. Learn in law school the tools to serve your clients well, and trust that society will compensate that excellent, personally-satisfying service.

I invite you to contact me at DrStipkala@gmail.com. I want to serve **you** better, so please give me feedback on this book. What was helpful? Was anything unclear? Do you have unanswered questions you hoped would be answered by this book? Help me help others similarly situated to you. I, and they, will be truly grateful.

Welcome, Dear Reader, to the exhilarating study of the Law!

92461509R00077

Made in the USA
Lexington, KY
05 July 2018